My School

Kenny Allen

REAL LIFE readers™

Rosen Classroom™

New York

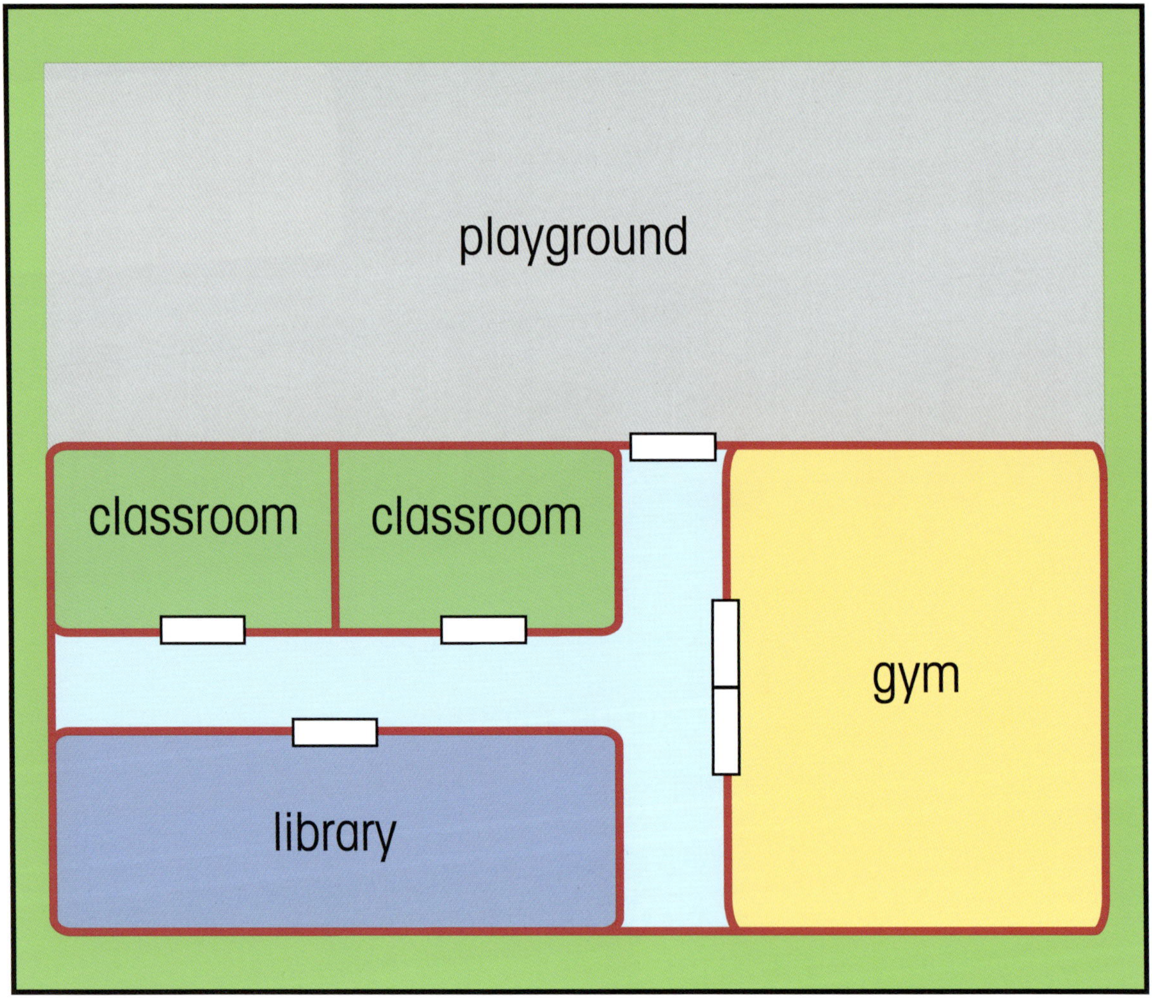

This is a map of
my school.

This is my classroom.

This is my gym.
We play here.

This is my library.
We read here.

This is my playground.
We play here.

What do you see around your school?

Words to Know

classroom

gym

library

playground

school